I Believe in Jesus

Leading Your Child to Christ

Lovingly dedicated to my
precious grandchildren.

Text copyright © 1999 by John MacArthur
Illustrations copyright © 1999 by Melinda MacArthur

All rights reserved.
No portion of this book may be reproduced in any form without the written
permission of the publisher, except for brief excerpts in reviews.

Published in Nashville, Tennessee, by Tommy Nelson™, a division
of Thomas Nelson, Inc.

Scripture quotations are from the *International Children's Bible*®, New
Century Version®, © 1983, 1986, 1988, 1999 by Tommy Nelson™, a division
of Thomas Nelson, Inc.

Library of Congress Cataloging-in-Publication Data
MacArthur, John, 1939-
     I believe in Jesus : leading your child to Christ / by John
MacArthur ; illustrations by Melinda MacArthur.
        p. cm.
     ISBN 0-8499-7541-7
     1. Theology, Doctrinal Juvenile literature. 2. Children Prayer—
books and devotions—English. I. Title.
BT77.M12 1999
249—dc21
                                                    99-23599
                                                       CIP

Printed in the United States of America
99 00 01 02 03 WCV 9 8 7 6 5 4 3 2 1

I Believe in Jesus

Leading Your Child to Christ

John MacArthur

Illustrated by Melinda MacArthur

Thomas Nelson, Inc.
Nashville

The Bible says that in the
beginning there was only God.
He has always been. God has no
beginning and no ending. There
were no sun, no stars, no planets,
no Earth—and no people. There
was just God. But He was not
alone, because God is really three
persons—God the Father, Jesus
the Son, and the Holy Spirit.
All three together are God.

**"The Lord God says, 'I am the
Alpha and the Omega. I am the
One who is and was and is
coming. I am the All-Powerful'"**

(Revelation 1:8).
Also see Matthew 28:19; John 1:1.

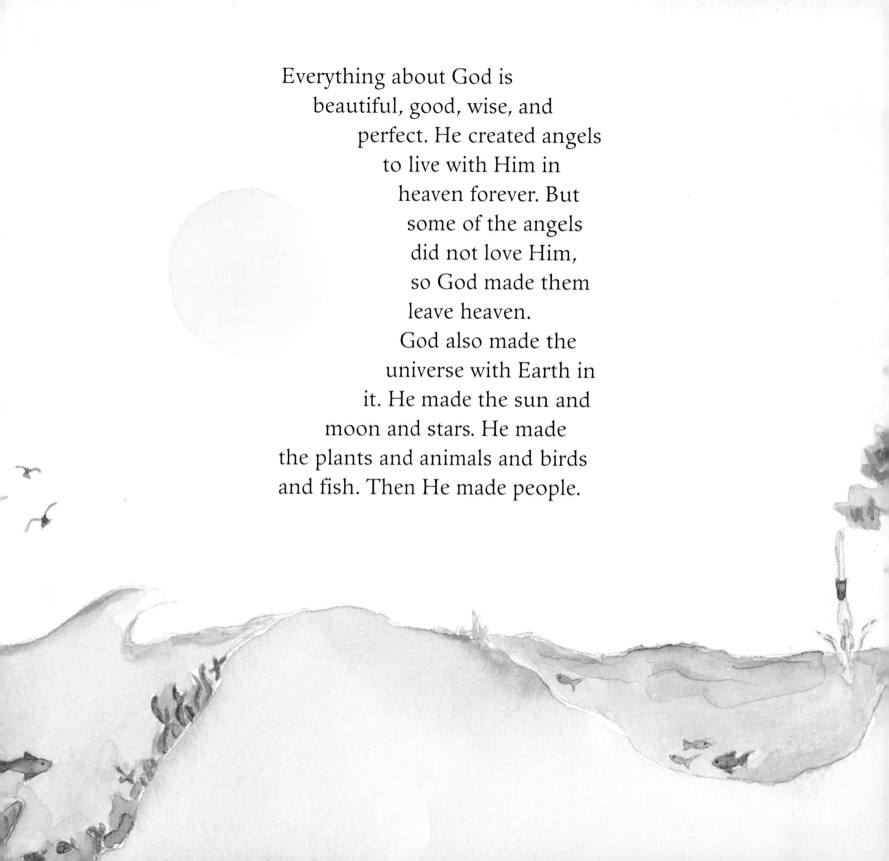

Everything about God is
beautiful, good, wise, and
perfect. He created angels
to live with Him in
heaven forever. But
some of the angels
did not love Him,
so God made them
leave heaven.
God also made the
universe with Earth in
it. He made the sun and
moon and stars. He made
the plants and animals and birds
and fish. Then He made people.

"In the beginning God created the sky and the earth" (Genesis 1:1).
". . . your Father in heaven is perfect" (Matthew 5:48). "God makes his angels. . . . All the angels are spirits who serve God and are sent to help those who will receive salvation" (Hebrews 1:7,14).

Also see Genesis 1:1–2:25; Revelation 12:8-9.

"There is no one without sin. None!"
. . . All people have sinned and are
not good enough for God's glory"
(Romans 3:10, 23).
"When someone sins, he earns what
sin pays—death" (Romans 6:23).

Also see Genesis 3:1-24.

The first man and woman God created were Adam and Eve. God gave them the beautiful Garden of Eden to live in. But a very sad thing happened. Adam and Eve disobeyed God. They let Satan, one of the bad angels, talk them into doing something God had told them not to do. God punished them by making them leave the garden. Their sins—all the bad things they did—had separated them from God. Every person born since Adam and Eve disobeys God, too. That is why all people die and should go to a place of punishment forever.

Have you ever noticed how hard it is to always be good, kind, loving, and unselfish? How hard it is to obey? How hard it is to always love God with all your heart? Well, like other people, sometimes you do bad things, too. God could leave you like that and punish you just as He did Adam and Eve and the bad angels. But because God loves people so much, He wants to fill His beautiful heaven with people who will live with Him forever. Our sin should keep us out of heaven, but instead, God invites everyone—you too!—to come to Him and ask for forgiveness for our sins. And He *promises* forgiveness to each one who asks.

"For God loved the world so much that he gave his only Son. God gave his Son so that whoever believes in him may not be lost, but have eternal life" (John 3:16).

Also see Romans 6:23;
Ephesians 1:7; 1 John 1:9.

"Lord, you are kind and forgiving. You have great love for those who call to you. Lord, hear my prayer. Listen when I ask for mercy" (Psalm 86:5–6).

Also see Psalm 103:8–18.

How can God just forgive us? Shouldn't He punish us? If God forgives us, does that mean that the bad things we do are not *really* that bad? No, they are bad! In fact, they are so bad that even though God forgives us and doesn't punish us, He still punishes every one of our sins. How can God punish our sins and not punish us? God always knows exactly what to do. He has a plan.

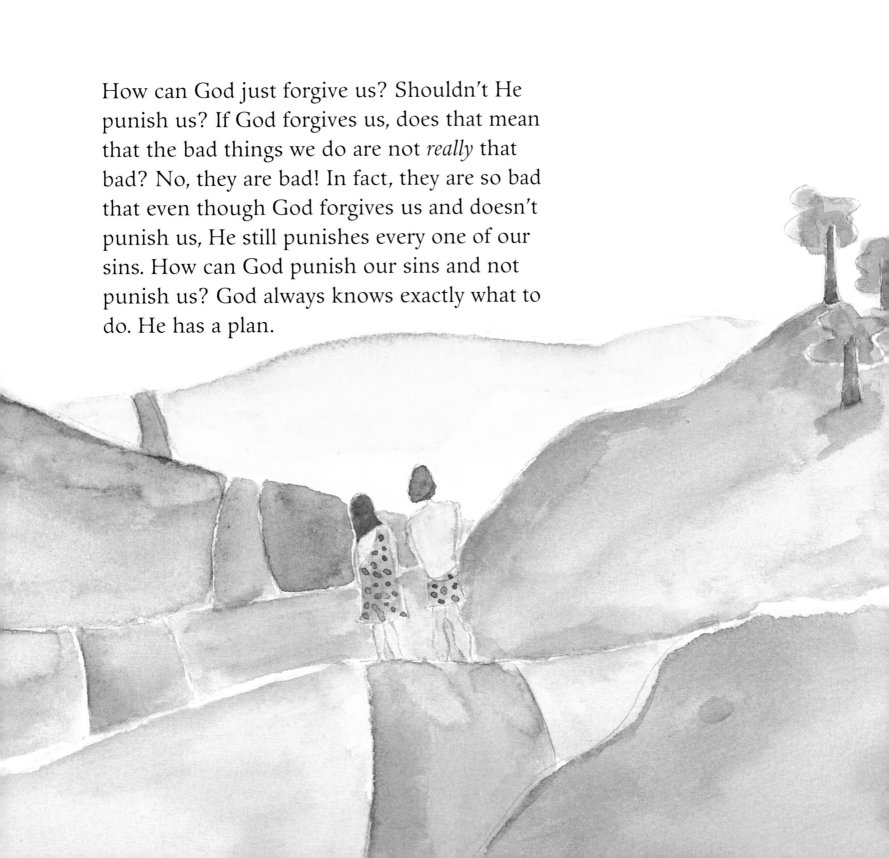

God's Son, Jesus, came to Earth to take the punishment for us. Jesus is One of the three persons who are God. And Jesus was willing to come down from heaven to become a real human like we are and to be punished for our sins. Jesus came to Earth as a baby. He was born to Mary and Joseph in a town called Bethlehem. He was born to die for us.

"But he was wounded for the wrong things we did. He was crushed for the evil things we did. The punishment, which made us well, was given to him. And we are healed because of his wounds. . . . The Lord has put on him the punishment for all the evil we have done" (Isaiah 53:5–6).

Also see Matthew 1:19–2:1; John 19:16–37.

Jesus grew up in a town called Nazareth. He preached about God and God's will. Everywhere Jesus went, He did miracles. He never thought, said, or did anything wrong. He never once displeased God. And He never sinned! Not even once. He did everything right all through His life, and God was totally pleased with Him.

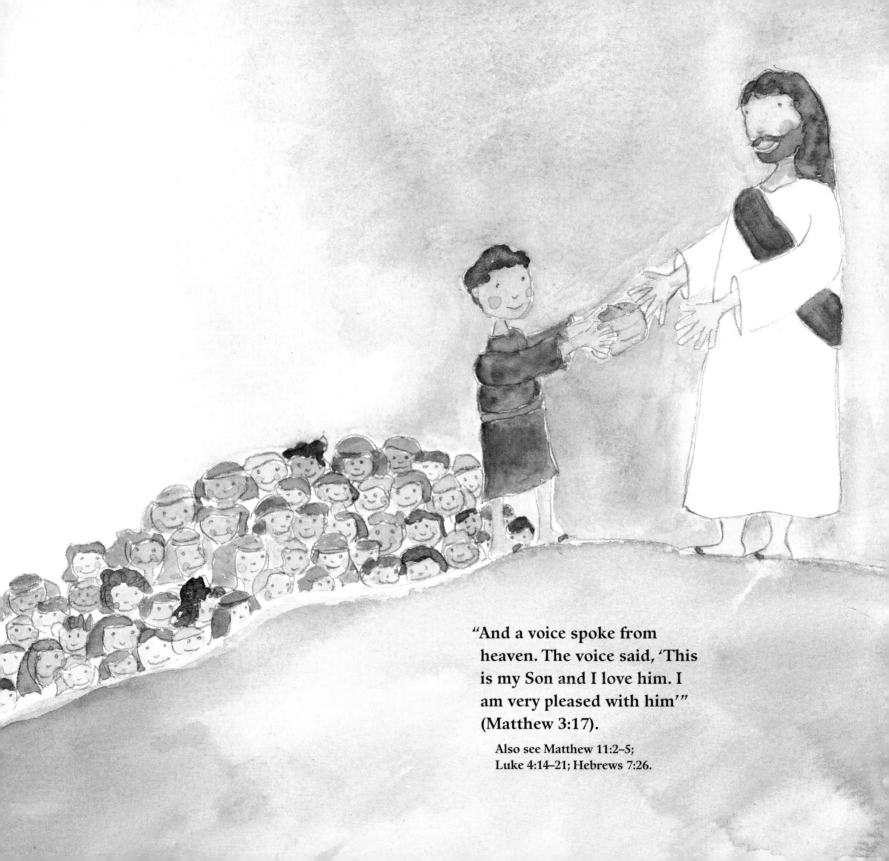

"And a voice spoke from heaven. The voice said, 'This is my Son and I love him. I am very pleased with him'" (Matthew 3:17).

Also see Matthew 11:2–5;
Luke 4:14–21; Hebrews 7:26.

Jesus is perfect. He didn't deserve to be punished. But He died on the cross to take on Himself the punishment that sinners deserve. Even though He had never even had one bad thought or said one mean word, He was punished as if He had done the worst sins anyone could ever do. Because He was given the punishment sinners deserve, God can now treat forgiven sinners as if they lived Jesus' perfect life.

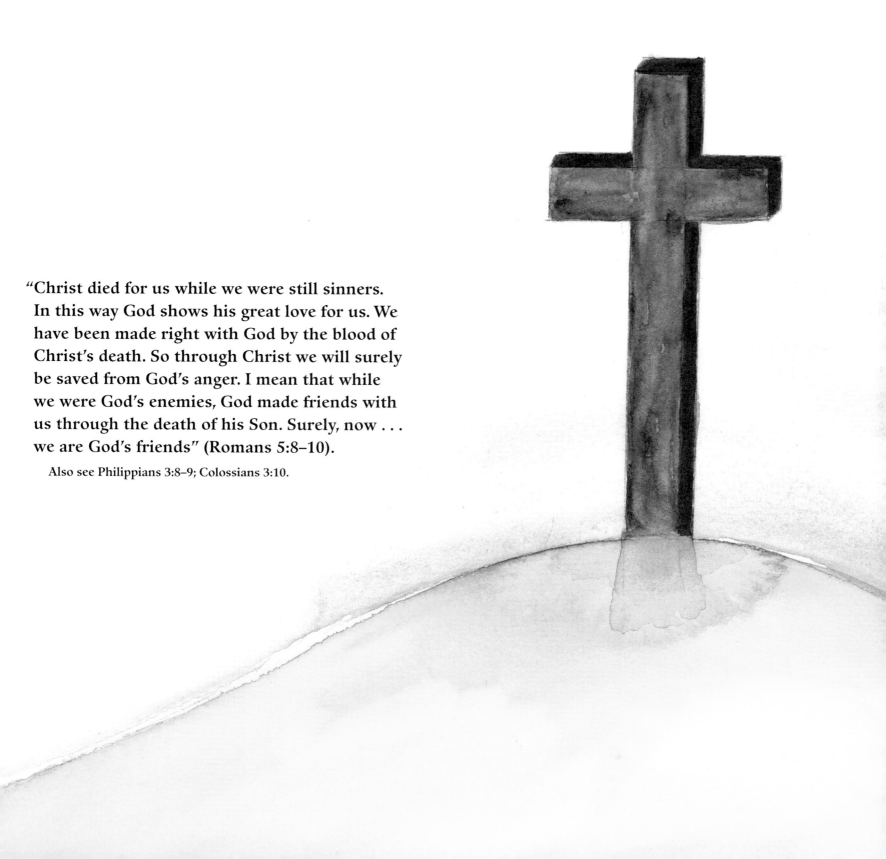

"Christ died for us while we were still sinners. In this way God shows his great love for us. We have been made right with God by the blood of Christ's death. So through Christ we will surely be saved from God's anger. I mean that while we were God's enemies, God made friends with us through the death of his Son. Surely, now . . . we are God's friends" (Romans 5:8–10).

Also see Philippians 3:8–9; Colossians 3:10.

"And this was the most important: that Christ died for our sins . . . that he was buried and was raised to life on the third day as the Scriptures say" (1 Corinthians 15:3–4).

Also see Matthew 28:1–10; Acts 1:9–11; Colossians 1:3–6; 1 Peter 1:4.

To complete His plan, God raised Jesus from the dead in three days. Soon after that, Jesus went back to heaven.

The best thing about being forgiven is that we don't have to be punished. Someday we can go to the amazing and wonderful place called heaven. This is a place where everyone is good, happy, loved, and peaceful forever.

You may be thinking, *How can God forgive me like that? Do I have to do something? Will it take a long time for God to forgive me? Do I have to be older?*

Listen. God will forgive you right now so that you can have a place in heaven.

It's His gift! He offers it to you!

Would you like God to forgive you so that someday you can live with Him in heaven? There are two words in the Bible that tell how this gift can be yours.

The first word is BELIEVE. Believe that Jesus alone could die for you and that He died so that God can forgive you for all the bad things you do. Believe that His dying was enough to pay for all your sins. Believe that He came back to life.

"If you use your mouth to say, 'Jesus is Lord,' and if you believe in your heart that God raised Jesus from death, then you will be saved. We believe with our hearts, and so we are made right with God. And we use our mouths to say that we believe, and so we are saved" (Romans 10:9–10).

The second word is RECEIVE. Receive Jesus as your Savior— the perfect One who was punished on the cross for the things sinful people do. That means telling Him you are sorry for the bad things you do. It means thanking Him for dying for sinners like you on the cross. It means telling Him that someday you want to live with Him in heaven with all the forgiven people. Receiving Jesus means telling Him that you want His special gift. You want Him to forgive you!

"But some people did accept him.
They believed in him. To them he gave
the right to become children of God.
They did not become his children in the
human way. They were not born because
of the desire or wish of some man. They
were born of God" (John 1:12–13).

Right now—bow your head. Tell Jesus that you believe in Him and what He did. Tell Him that you want to receive Him as your own Savior. Ask Jesus to forgive you for the times when you disobey. For the times when you are unkind and selfish. For everything you do that makes Him unhappy.

"If we say we have no sin, we are
  fooling ourselves, and the truth is
  not in us. But if we confess our sins,
  he will forgive our sins. We can trust
  God. He does what is right. He will
  make us clean from all the wrongs
  we have done" (1 John 1:8–9).
"Believe in the Lord Jesus and you
  will be saved . . ." (Acts 16:31).

If you asked honestly, you can trust God to forgive you! Keep trusting Him from now on. You show that you accept God's forgiveness by being baptized and obeying His Word.

Jesus will be your friend forever. Someday, He will take you to heaven to live with our amazing God.

"The Father gives me my people. Every one of them will come to me, and I will always accept them. . . . Everyone who sees the Son and believes in him has eternal life" (John 6:37,40).

Also see John 14:1–6.

The Holy Spirit is the other of the three who are God. He will come to live inside you and help you to love God. He will help you obey God and praise Him.

"You should know that your body is a temple for the Holy Spirit. The Holy Spirit is in you. You have received the Holy Spirit from God. You do not own yourselves. You were bought by God for a price. So honor God. . . ." (1 Corinthians 6:19–20).

Also see Galatians 5:22; Ephesians 1:13-14.

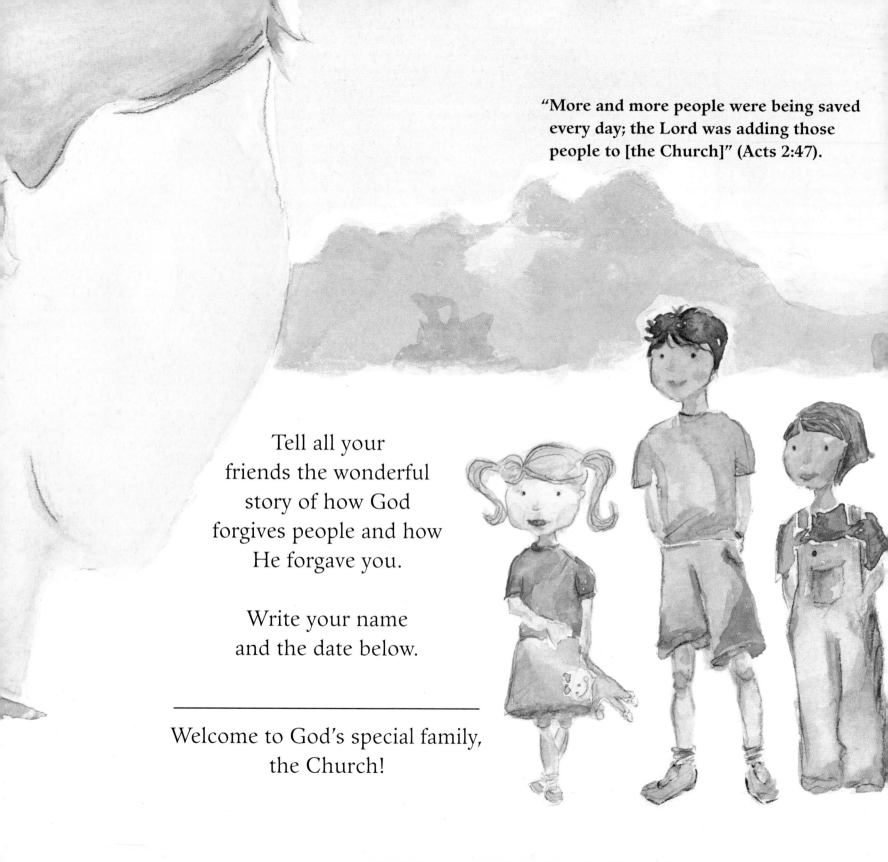

"More and more people were being saved every day; the Lord was adding those people to [the Church]" (Acts 2:47).

Tell all your friends the wonderful story of how God forgives people and how He forgave you.

Write your name and the date below.

_____

Welcome to God's special family, the Church!